Printed in the United States
by Baker & Taylor Publisher Services

Instructions

Cook macaroni with salted water al dente and according to pkg. directions. Drain pasta and set aside.

Melt butter in deep saucepan large enough to hold all ingredients.

Whisk in flour over low heat until smooth

Gradually whisk in milk, stirring constantly.

Sprinkle in the cheeses, continuing to stir for several minutes until cheeses are melted.

Stir in salt, pepper and hot sauce. Sauce will get thicker.

Add the cooked pasta to the sauce and combine until the pasta is thoroughly coated. The mixture will have a lot of sauce but the pasta will absorb some of it when baked.

Pour into a sprayed or buttered 3 qt. baking dish.

In a small bowl combine the Panko crumbs, melted butter and Parmesan cheese.

Sprinkle over the top and bake in preheated 375 degree oven for 20 to 30 minutes. Mac and Cheese should be bubbly and golden brown.

ENJOY!!

Mimi's Mac and Cheese

Creamy, outrageously cheesy, using three different cheeses with a crunchy Parmesan topping everyone loves.

Ingredients

16 oz. elbow Macaroni
1 tsp. Salt

8 tbsp. Butter
½ cup all purpose Flour
4 cups whole Milk
4 cups shredded Extra Sharp Cheddar Cheese (12 oz.)
2 cups shredded Gruyere or Swiss cheese(6oz.)
½ cup grated Parmesan Cheese
several drops Hot Sauce such as Tabasco – to taste
Salt and Pepper

1 cup Panko Crumbs
4 tbsp. melted Butter
2/3 cup grated Parmesan Cheese

About the Family

The Marshall family lives on the beautiful Eastern Shore of Virginia. This entrepreneur family has started many businesses, the latest being Cape Charles Brewing Company.

The matriarch of the family is Deborah or more often called Mimi and says she could not have raised six children without peanut butter and Mac and Cheese. It became *Mimi's Mac and Cheese* with the arrival of grandchildren and great grandchildren. It is even on the menu at the brewery.

Artistic talent also runs in the family and two of the granddaughters, twins Hayley and Alex, wanted to put together some drawings for the book and their mother Meg joined in. *I Love Macaroni and Cheese* became a collaborative effort.

The family hopes you will enjoy this happy book and they've also included a recipe for *Mimi's Mac and Cheese*. ENJOY!!

I surely know that I would be
The happiest kid you'd ever see
if Mac and Cheese were friends with me

My mom says I am silly
to love this food so much,
but when you think about it
it's got the Midas touch.

When I am sleeping soundly
In the middle of the night
My dreams are quite delicious
They're full of cheesy bites

Even for my birthday
and its time to celebrate
My favorite wish is for my favorite dish
A Mac and Cheese birthday cake

When my friends come over to play
They hope that they'll be asked to stay
For Mac and Cheese, that lip-smacking treat
The scrumptious food kids love to eat

If Mac and Cheese were dinner's plan

I'd sail the deep, blue ocean

Or trek the desert sand

I'd climb the snowy mountain

Whenever I'm unhappy
Cause things are upside down
I think of my most favorite food
It takes away the frown

I Love it on a sandwich
or on top of Mom's apple pie
But the best way that I Love it
Is piled up very high!

I eat it from my breakfast bowl
or from my dinner plate.
If it spills down upon the floor
I still think it tastes great

I Love it in the morning time
I Love it in the night
I Love it more and more and more
with each big, cheesy bite!

I just
LOVE
Macaroni and Cheese!

For Matthew Dooley
and all children
who savor Mac and Cheese
with gleeful delight.

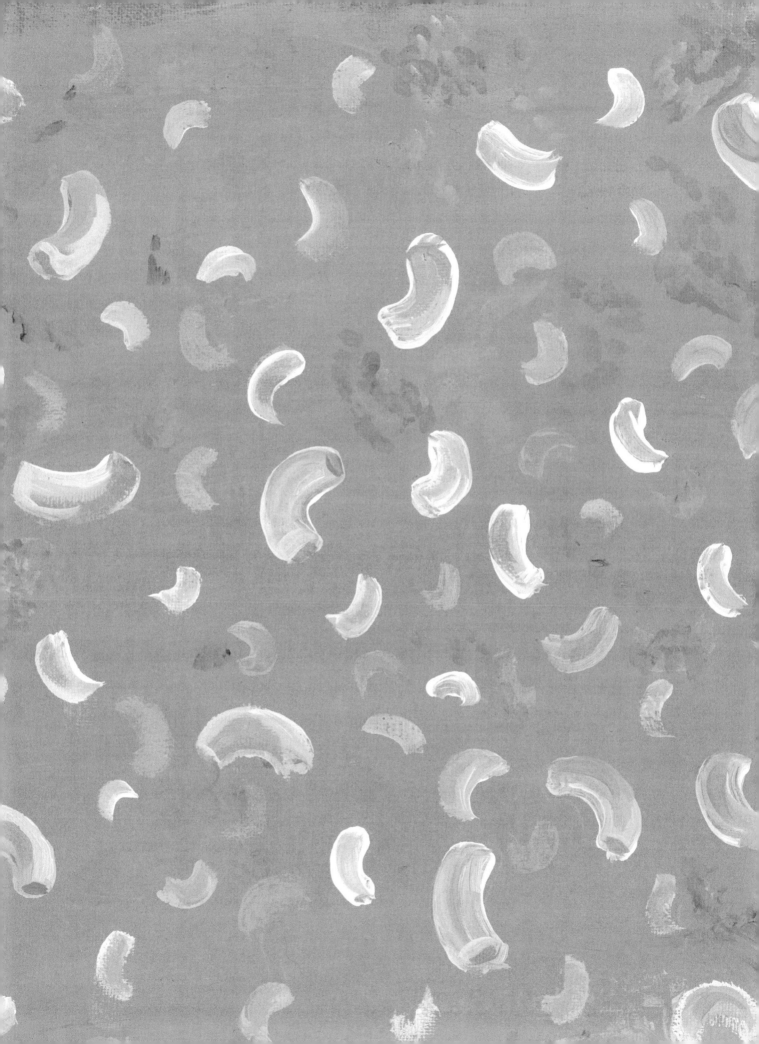

i Love Macaroni and Cheese

Written by Deborah L. Marshall

Illustrated by Hayley Marshall, Alex Marshall, Meg Marshall

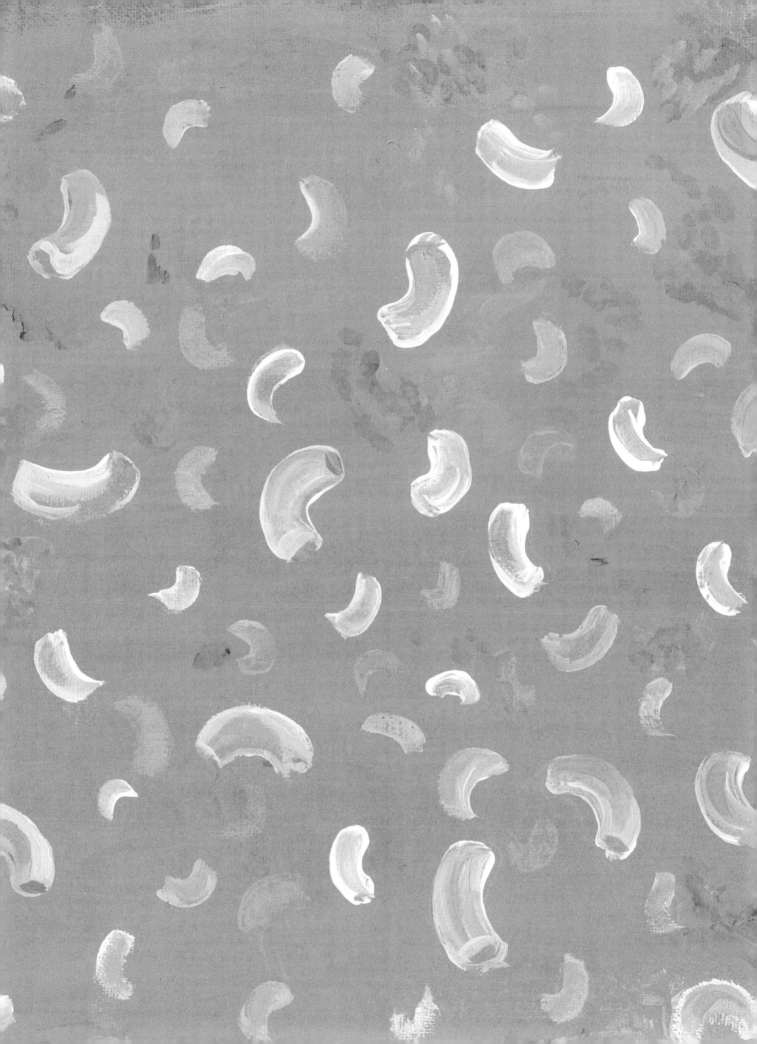

AuthorHouse™
1663 Liberty Drive
Bloomington, IN 47403
www.authorhouse.com
Phone: 833-262-8899

This book is printed on acid-free paper.

ISBN: 978-1-7283-2536-1 (hc)
ISBN: 978-1-7283-2534-7 (e)

Library of Congress Control Number: 2019912999

Print information available on the last page.

Published by AuthorHouse 10/30/2021

authorHOUSE®